LANDMARK TOP TENS

The World's Most Amazing
Skyscrapers

Michael Hurley

Chicago, Illinois

www.heinemannraintree.com
Visit our website to find out more information about Heinemann-Raintree books.

To order:
☎ Phone 888-454-2279
💻 Visit www.heinemannraintree.com to browse our catalog and order online.

© 2012 Raintree
an imprint of Capstone Global Library, LLC
Chicago, Illinois

Customer Service: 888-454-2279
Visit our website at www.heinemannraintree.com

Edited by Megan Cotugno and Laura Knowles
Designed by Victoria Allen
Original illustrations © Capstone Global Library Ltd (2011)
Illustrated by HL Studios and Oxford Designers and Illustrators
Picture research by Hannah Taylor and Ruth Blair
Production by Camilla Crask
Originated by Capstone Global Library Ltd
Printed and bound in the United States of America, North Mankato, MN
15 14 13 12 11
10 9 8 7 6 5 4 3 2

Library of Congress Cataloging-in-Publication Data
Hurley, Michael, 1979-
  The world's most amazing skyscrapers / Michael Hurley.—1st ed.
       p. cm.—(Landmark top tens)
  Includes bibliographical references and index.
  ISBN 978-1-4109-4242-5—ISBN 978-1-4109-4253-1 1.
Skyscrapers—Juvenile literature. I. Title.
  NA6230.H87 2011
  720.483—dc22   2010038408

092011
006318RP

Acknowledgments
The author and publishers are grateful to the following for permission to reproduce copyright material: Alamy Images pp. 8 (© David Wall), 25 (© Eric Bchtold); Corbis pp. 10 (Sergio Dorantes), 11 (Bertrand Gardel), 14 (Reuters/Mosab Omar), 15 (epa/Ali Haider), 16 (George Hammerstein), 21 (Derek M. Allan); Getty Images pp. 7 (Science & Society Picture Library), 18 (AFP); istockphoto p. 23 (© Dmitry Mordvintsev); Photolibrary pp. 17 (Robert Harding), 24 (imagebroker), 5, 13, 20; Shutterstock pp. 6 (© jovannig), 9 (© Guido Amrein, Switzerland), 12 (© MACHKAZU), 19 (© ssuaphotos), 22 (© cloki), 4 (© Songquan Deng).

Cover photograph of the Petronas Towers, Kuala Lumpur, Malaysia reproduced with permission of Alamy Images (© Roussel Bernard).

We would like to thank Daniel Block for his invaluable help in the preparation of this book.

Every effort has been made to contact copyright holders of material reproduced in this book. Any omissions will be rectified in subsequent printings if notice is given to the publisher.

Disclaimer
All the internet addresses (URLs) given in this book were valid at the time of going to press. However, due to the dynamic nature of the internet, some addresses may have changed, or sites may have changed or ceased to exist since publication. While the author and publisher regret any inconvenience this may cause readers, no responsibility for any such changes can be accepted by either the author or the publisher.

Contents

Some words are printed in bold, **like this**. You can find out what they mean in the glossary.

Very tall buildings are called skyscrapers because they are so tall that they look as if they are touching the sky. The first skyscrapers were built in the United States at the end of the 1800s. One of the first examples was the Home Insurance Building in Chicago. It was made using concrete and steel. The Woolworth Building in New York City, completed in 1913, was 793 feet (242 meters) tall.

Taller and taller

During the 1930s more skyscrapers were built. As technology has improved, skyscrapers have become taller and taller. Skyscrapers are often built in areas where there is a high population but not much land to build on. Skyscrapers allow **architects** to create homes, offices, and hotels that can accommodate many people.

The New York City **skyline** is famous all over the world.

The amazing Jin Mao Tower in Shanghai, is the second tallest building in China.

The Empire State Building in New York City is probably the most famous skyscraper in the world. When it was built in 1931, it was the tallest building that had ever been constructed. It held the record as the tallest building in the world until 1972.

The Empire State Building is a famous New York City landmark.

Empire State Building
Location: New York City, New York
Height: 1,250 feet (381 meters)
That's Amazing!
More than 100 movies have featured the Empire State Building, including *Independence Day* (1998) and *King Kong* (2005).

The construction workers on the Empire State Building had to work hundreds of feet above the ground without any safety equipment!

New York view

Ten million bricks were used to build the Empire State Building. It took construction workers 18 months to build. It has 102 floors and is 1,250 feet (381 meters) high. There are 1,860 steps from the street to the 102nd floor. The Empire State Building **observatory** has more than 3.5 million visitors every year.

The Q1 Tower is the tallest skyscraper in Australia. It was built on the Gold Coast, an area of Queensland in the northeast of the country. This skyscraper dominates the Gold Coast **skyline**. The name Q1 is short for Queensland Number One.

The Q1 Tower really stands out among the smaller buildings along the Australian Gold Coast.

Q1 Tower

Location: Gold Coast, Queensland, Australia

Height: 1,058 feet (322.5 meters)

That's Amazing!
The Q1 Tower has a swimming pool on the 74th floor. It is the highest swimming pool in Australia!

Heavy spire

The Q1 Tower took three years to build and was completed in 2005. It has 78 floors and the total height of the building, including the spire, is 1,058 feet (322.5 meters). The spire weighs an amazing 121 tons. The Q1 Tower has the fastest elevators in Australia. They travel at over 20 mph (32.4 kmph).

Bright Lights

The lights at the top of the Q1 Tower are so bright they can be seen from 124 miles (200 kilometers) away.

The stunning and **imposing** Petronas Towers in Malaysia were the world's tallest skyscrapers from 1998 until 2004. The towers are 1,483 feet (452 meters) tall with 88 floors, and took six years to build. These impressive skyscrapers reflected the growth of the Malaysian **economy** at the time. The Petronas Towers are used mainly as offices, with a huge shopping mall on the ground floor.

What Does Petronas Mean?

Petronas is short for "Petroliam Nasional," the Malaysian national petroleum company. The Petronas Company occupies all of Tower 1.

The Petronas Towers during construction. When they were completed they became the tallest buildings in Malaysia.

The Petronas Towers look amazing. They are the fourth tallest skyscrapers in the world.

Petronas Towers

Location: Kuala Lumpur, Malaysia

Height: 1,483 feet (452 meters)

That's Amazing!
These towers have an incredible 32,000 windows!

Amazing views

The Petronas Towers are two skyscrapers that are connected by a **skywalk** on the 42nd floor. The towers are called Petronas Tower 1 and Petronas Tower 2. The skywalk has a viewing area that is open to the public. If you're not scared of heights, there is a great view of the city of Kuala Lumpur up there!

Taipei 101 in Taiwan is the second-tallest skyscraper in the world. It is 1,670 feet (509 meters) tall and has 101 floors. It took six years to build and was completed in 2004. The design of the building is **inspired** by traditional Chinese **architecture**. The shape looks like a pagoda, a traditional Asian building. The sectioned tower was inspired by the bamboo plant, a Chinese symbol of strength, **resilience**, and elegance.

Taipei 101
Location: Taipei, Taiwan
Height: 1,670 feet (509 meters)
That's Amazing!
This skyscraper has the fastest elevators in the world. It only takes 43 seconds to reach the top! The brakes on the elevators are **ceramic**, not steel, for better stopping power.

Taipei 101 dominates the skyline in Taiwan.

Multiuse building

Taipei 101 is used for many different things. Seventy-seven of the floors are office space. There are restaurants and stores on other floors. There is also a two-floor gym. Beneath the building is a station for the Taipei Mass Rapid Transit train.

Stopping the Sway

A large, very heavy ball called a tuned mass damper (below) hangs inside Taipei 101. It helps to keep the building from swaying in high winds or in an earthquake. It works like a pendulum, swinging in the opposite direction to the movement of the building.

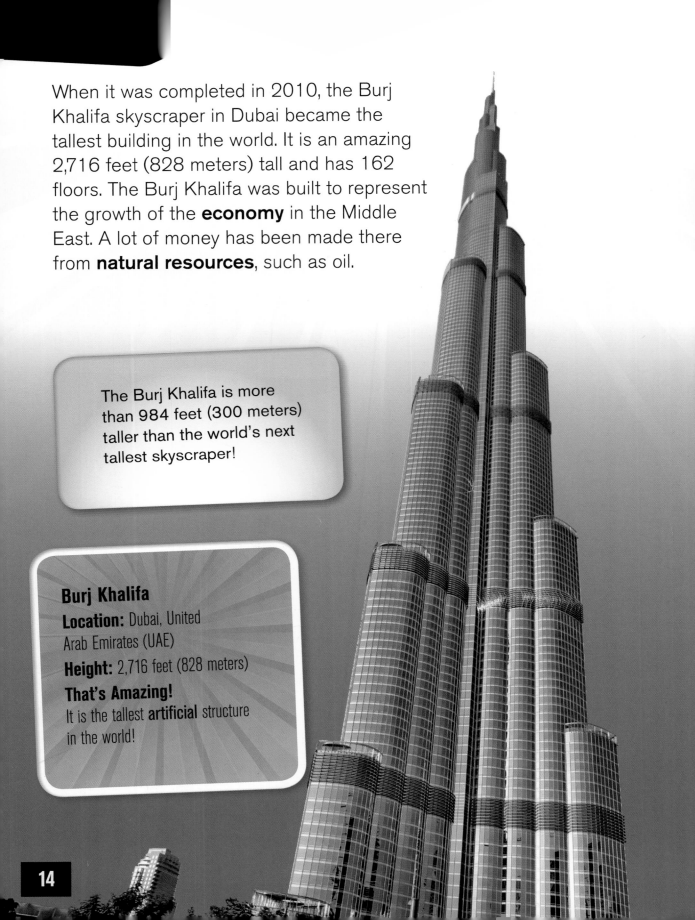

When it was completed in 2010, the Burj Khalifa skyscraper in Dubai became the tallest building in the world. It is an amazing 2,716 feet (828 meters) tall and has 162 floors. The Burj Khalifa was built to represent the growth of the **economy** in the Middle East. A lot of money has been made there from **natural resources**, such as oil.

The Burj Khalifa is more than 984 feet (300 meters) taller than the world's next tallest skyscraper!

Burj Khalifa

Location: Dubai, United Arab Emirates (UAE)

Height: 2,716 feet (828 meters)

That's Amazing!
It is the tallest **artificial** structure in the world!

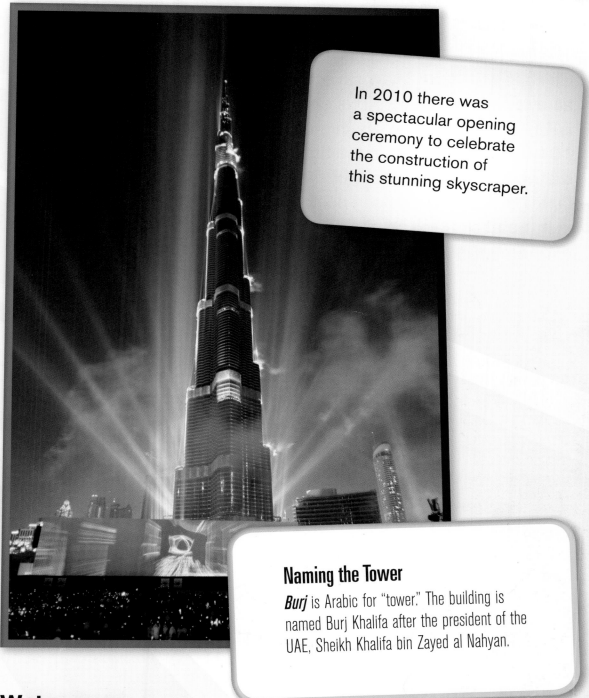

In 2010 there was a spectacular opening ceremony to celebrate the construction of this stunning skyscraper.

Naming the Tower

Burj is Arabic for "tower." The building is named Burj Khalifa after the president of the UAE, Sheikh Khalifa bin Zayed al Nahyan.

Water reuse

This skyscraper is so massive that the **condensation** from the air-conditioning system creates enough water to fill 20 Olympic-sized swimming pools each year. This water is used for the large gardens surrounding the base of the tower.

Shanghai World Financial Center

The Shanghai World Financial Center in China is an extraordinary skyscraper with an eye-catching design. This skyscraper is 1,614 feet (492 meters) high and has 101 floors. It was built in the **financial district** of Shanghai. Many of the world's tallest buildings have been built recently in this part of China, as the country's **economy** has grown.

Shanghai World Financial Center

Location: Shanghai, China
Height: 1,614 feet (492 meters)

That's Amazing!
This skyscraper has the highest observation deck in the world!

Many of the newest and tallest skyscrapers in China can be found in Shanghai.

Huge hole in the building!

Near the top of the building there is a huge **trapezoidal**-shaped hole. This 50 foot- (15 meter-) diameter hole was made to reduce wind pressure on the building. The hole allows air to pass through the building instead of pushing against it. It is a very unusual and dramatic design, but also very useful!

Foundation Stone

The **foundation stone** was laid in 1997, but the building was not completed until 2008. The delay was caused by financial problems.

The Shanghai World Financial Center looks amazing. It is the tallest building in China, and the third-tallest skyscraper in the world.

Willis Tower

Willis Tower in Chicago, Illinois is the tallest skyscraper in the United States. It was designed using nine box shapes. Each huge box is 75 feet (23 meters) wide. Two boxes are 50 floors high, two are 66 floors high, three are 90 floors high, and two are an incredible 108 floors high.

Plumbing and Wiring

Willis Tower contains 25,000 miles (40,234 kilometers) of plumbing and 2,000 miles (3,219 kilometers) of electrical wire!

Willis Tower
Location: Chicago, Illinois
Height: 1,450 feet (442 meters)
That's Amazing!
Willis Tower has 104 elevators!

Chicago is famous for its very tall buildings. Some of them were built at the beginning of the 20th century. The most recent was completed in 2009.

Twenty-two towering years

Willis Tower, once known as Sears Tower, was built between 1972 and 1974. It was the world's tallest building for 22 years. It is 1,450 feet (442 meters) tall and has 108 floors. There is an observation deck for visitors on the 103rd floor. The elevators that go up to this deck are some of the fastest in the world. They can move at speeds of 18.1 mph (29.2 kmph).

Central Plaza is one of the most eye-catching of all of the famous skyscrapers in Hong Kong. This skyscraper was built in 1992. It is 1,227 feet (374 meters) tall and has 78 floors. It was the tallest building in Hong Kong for seven years. For four years, it also held the record as the tallest building in Asia.

Hong Kong has one of the most dramatic **skylines** in the world.

Central Plaza
Location: Hong Kong, China
Height: 1,227 feet (374 meters)
That's Amazing!
This is the second-tallest concrete structure in the world!

Expensive land

Hong Kong is a small place with a big population. There are only 403 square miles (1,042 square kilometers) of land and 7 million people. The land is very expensive, and most of the buildings are multistory. When Central Plaza was built, the land cost three times as much as the construction of the skyscraper!

These construction workers are building the skyscraper's roof, 78 stories above the ground!

Highest Church

The top floor of Central Plaza contains a church. It is the highest church in the world.

The City of Capitals skyscraper in Moscow is the tallest skyscraper in Europe. It is 991 feet (302 meters) tall and has 76 floors. The City of Capitals is actually two interconnecting buildings that were completed in 2010.

The City of Capitals was constructed in concrete and glass using an unusual irregular "building blocks" design.

City of Capitals
Location: Moscow, Russia
Height: 991 feet (302 meters)
That's Amazing!
This skyscraper is the tallest building in Europe.

This spectacular group of modern buildings overlooking Moscow includes the City of Capitals (right).

First for Russia

The City of Capitals was the first building in Russia to be built more than 984 feet (300 meters) tall.

Two capital cities

The two buildings of the City of Capitals have been named after the current and former capital cities of Russia. One building is called Moscow and the other is called St. Petersburg. It is very modern-looking compared to many of the other buildings in Moscow, and contains office space, apartments, stores, restaurants, and a gym.

The Chrysler Building in New York City was the first skyscraper in the world to stand more than 984 feet (300 meters) tall. The building was completed in 1930 and was the world's tallest building for one year—before the Empire State Building was completed. These two New York City skyscrapers represented the wealth in the United States at that time.

The Chrysler Building was built in 1930, but looks like a modern, 21st-century skyscraper.

Chrysler Building
Location: New York City, New York
Height: 1,047 feet (319 meters)
That's Amazing!
It is the tallest **brick-clad** structure in the world.

Stunning building

The Chrysler Building is a stunning skyscraper. It was built using more than 21,000 tons of steel and nearly 4 million bricks. The Chrysler Motor Company built this skyscraper and used it as the company headquarters for 20 years. The skyscraper keeps its name because it is such an **iconic** building. It is recognized all over the world.

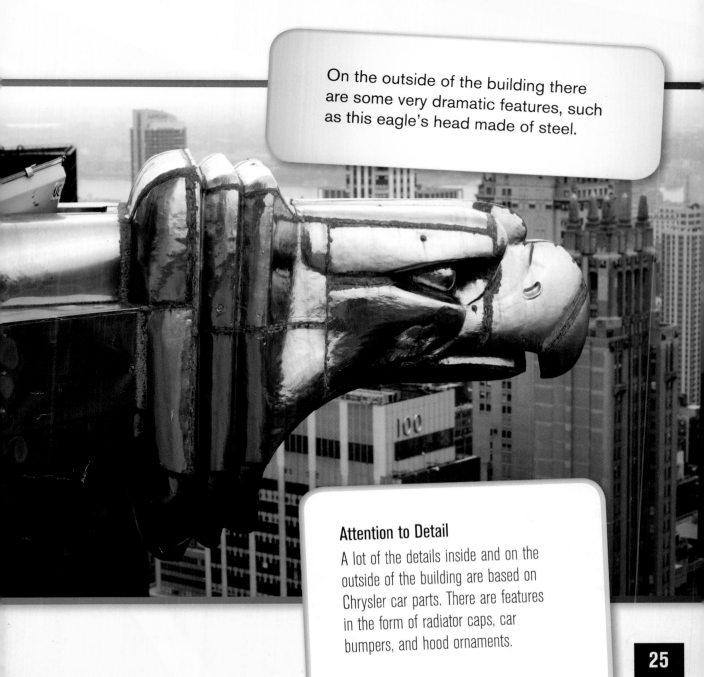

On the outside of the building there are some very dramatic features, such as this eagle's head made of steel.

Attention to Detail

A lot of the details inside and on the outside of the building are based on Chrysler car parts. There are features in the form of radiator caps, car bumpers, and hood ornaments.

Many skyscrapers are being designed and built all over the world today. Taller and more spectacular skyscrapers have been built in the Middle East and Asia in recent years. Many of the buildings currently under construction will be among the world's tallest skyscrapers. Skyscrapers being built in London and in Germany will compete to be the tallest building in Europe.

This diagram shows some of the world's most amazing skyscrapers.

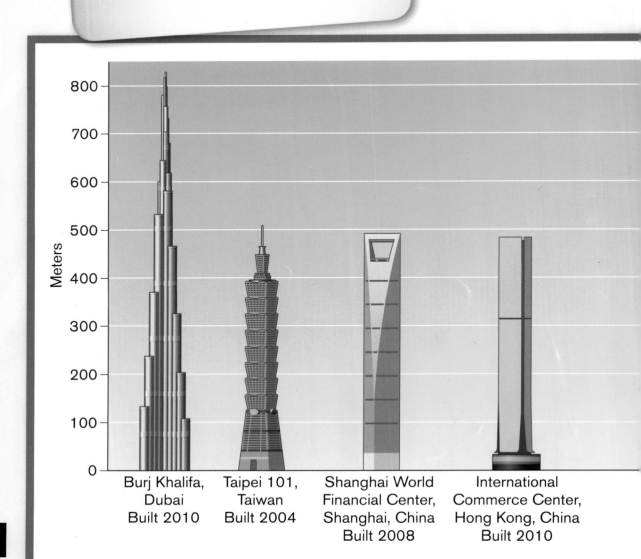

New skyscrapers

After the tragic events of September 11, 2001, when two planes flew into the World Trade Center in New York City, the construction of skyscrapers has been carefully reviewed. New skyscrapers are built with clearer emergency exits and wider stairwells. Some skyscrapers even have elevators on the outside in case of an emergency.

Environmental impact

Architects who design new skyscrapers also need to consider the impact on the environment. Some new skyscrapers are built with solar panels that use the Sun's energy to generate electricity. These panels can reduce the amount of fuel used to heat these huge buildings.

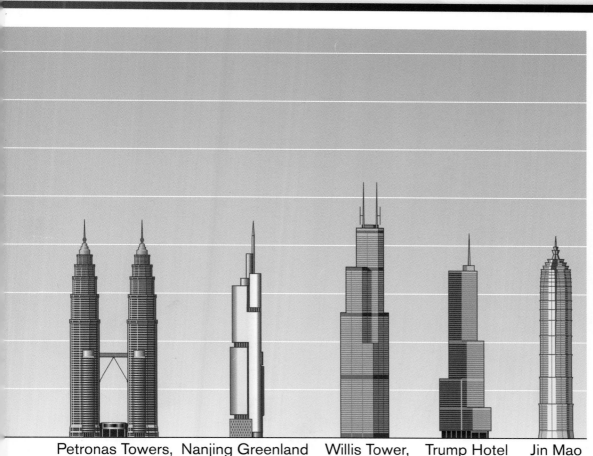

Petronas Towers, Kuala Lumpur, Malaysia
Built 1998

Nanjing Greenland Financial Complex, Nanjing, China
Built 2010

Willis Tower, Chicago, United States
Built 1974

Trump Hotel and Tower, Chicago, United States
Built 2009

Jin Mao Tower, Shanghai, China
Built 1998

Skyscraper Facts and Figures

There are skyscrapers in most major cities in the world. Some of these skyscrapers are so tall that you cannot see the top when you look up at them from the ground. Which skyscraper do you think is the most amazing?

Empire State Building

Location: New York City, New York

Height: 1,250 feet (381 meters)

That's Amazing!
More than 100 movies have featured the Empire State Building, including *Independence Day* (1998) and *King Kong* (2005).

Q1 Tower

Location: Gold Coast, Queensland, Australia

Height: 1,058 feet (322.5 meters)

That's Amazing!
The Q1 Tower has a swimming pool on the 74th floor. It is the highest swimming pool in Australia!

Petronas Towers

Location: Kuala Lumpur, Malaysia

Height: 1,483 feet (452 meters)

That's Amazing!
These towers have an incredible 32,000 windows!

Taipei 101

Location: Taipei, Taiwan

Height: 1,670 feet (509 meters)

That's Amazing!
This skyscraper has the fastest elevators in the world. It only takes 43 seconds to reach the top! The brakes on the elevators are **ceramic**, not steel, for better stopping power.

Burj Khalifa

Location: Dubai, United Arab Emirates (UAE)

Height: 2,716 feet (828 meters)

That's Amazing!
It is the tallest **artificial** structure in the world!

Shanghai World Financial Center

Location: Shanghai, China

Height: 1,614 feet (492 meters)

That's Amazing!
This skyscraper has the highest observation deck in the world!

Willis Tower

Location: Chicago, Illinois

Height: 1,450 feet (442 meters)

That's Amazing!
Willis Tower has 104 elevators!

Central Plaza

Location: Hong Kong, China

Height: 1,227 feet (374 meters)

That's Amazing!
This is the second-tallest concrete structure in the world!

City of Capitals

Location: Moscow, Russia

Height: 991 feet (302 meters)

That's Amazing!
This skyscraper is the tallest building in Europe.

Chrysler Building

Location: New York City, New York

Height: 1,047 feet (319 meters)

That's Amazing!
It is the tallest **brick-clad** structure in the world.

architect person who designs a building

architecture style of a building

artificial made by humans

brick-clad building that has an outer layer of bricks

ceramic nonmetal material that is tough and heat-resistant

condensation water that forms on a cold surface, such as a window, when it comes into contact with warmer air

economy production and use of goods and services that create money for a country

financial district area of a city where banks and money markets are found

foundation stone stone laid in a ceremony to celebrate the start of a building

iconic something that is famous and significant to many people

imposing something that appears very grand

inspired influenced by

natural resource material that occurs in nature that can be used by humans, for example coal and oil

observatory place where you can view something

resilience ability to recover quickly from a setback

skywalk walkway that connects two towers

skyline outline of buildings against the sky

trapezoidal four-sided with two parallel sides

Find Out More

Books

Bullard, Lisa. *The Empire State Building*. Minneapolis, Minn.: Lerner, 2010.

Curlee, Lynn. *Skyscraper*. New York, NY: Atheneum Books for Young Readers, 2007.

Franchino, Vicky. *How Did They Build That? Skyscraper*. Ann Arbor, Mich.: Cherry Lake, 2010.

Macken, JoAnn Early. *Building a Skyscraper*. Mankato, Minn.: Capstone, 2008.

Price, Sean. *The Story Behind Skyscrapers*. Chicago, IL: Heinemann Library, 2009.

Websites

http://kids.yahoo.com
Search for "bridges," "stadiums," and "skyscrapers" to find interesting facts as well as links to other useful sites.

http://www.pbs.org/wgbh/buildingbig
Explore large structures, and what it takes to build them, including skyscrapers and bridges.

http://www.emporis.com/application/?nav=skyscrapers_top1000&lng=3
The Emporis website features a list of the tallest skyscrapers in the world.

Index